DISCOVERING CAPTIVES

A GUIDE TO FORMING AND PERFECTING YOUR OWN INSURANCE COMPANY

DISCOVERING CAPTIVES

A GUIDE TO FORMING AND PERFECTING YOUR OWN INSURANCE COMPANY

Michael A. DiMayo, CFP®, CLU, ChFC
Kevin E. Myers, CPA, M.S. Taxation

DISCOVERING CAPTIVES

ISBN 978-0-9887301-0-6
Printed in the USA

Cover and Interior Design: Stepforward Creative
www.stepforwardnow.com

"The heart and soul of the company
is creativity and innovation."

- **Robert Iger,**
Chairman and Chief Executive, The Walt Disney Company

"Individual commitment to a group effort—
That is what makes a team work, a company work,
a society work, a civilization work."

- **Vince Lombardi,**
Hall of Fame Coach

"We are what we repeatedly do.
Excellence then, is not an act, but a habit."

- **Aristotle,**
Greek Philosopher

CONTENTS

ACKNOWLEDGEMENTS

Publishing and Marketing

The authors would like to thank Lisa and Glenn Roeca, Principals of Stepforward Creative, Towson, MD, for their incredible support and investment in both time and energy to help make this book possible. The contributions made by their seasoned, award winning collection of creative specialists was instrumental to the *Discovering Captives* project.

Contributions and Guidance

We would like to acknowledge the following people and organizations for their contributions throughout the writing of this book, which would not have been possible without their tireless support, encouragement and assistance:

Dick Goff, Managing Member, The Taft Companies, LLC.

Jeffrey K. Simpson, Director, Gordon, Fournaris & Mammarella, P.A.

Andrew Rennick, Associate, Gordon, Fournaris & Mammarella, P.A.

Others Providing Support

Douglas Bentle, Senior V.P., Impact Partnership; Pete Debany, Retired Bond Trader, Wolfe & Hurst, Inc.; Ellen DiMayo, President, Insurance Alternatives, Inc.; Joe Jankowski, Managing Partner, Armada Business Solutions; David Kirby, President, DKI Public

Relations; Daniel J. Kusaila, CPA, Tax Partner, Saslow, Lufkin & Buggy, LLP; Marianne Kuta, Investment Advisor; Craig C. Longenecker, DDS, Hereford Dental Health; Joanne Kenney Shaver, CPA, Principal, Cover & Rossiter, P.A.; James Stevenson, Chief Financial Officer, ABS Capital Partners; Harold S. Watt, Retired Engineer, Department of Defense.

We would also like to acknowledge everyone on the Oxford Team for the professionalism, creativity, dedication and long hours invested in this project. In this endeavor, as in all projects they take on throughout the year, our team again proved a relentless pursuit of excellence.

There were many others, including family and friends, who contributed to and provided input for this book, too numerous to mention. But, you know who you are.

Last, but not least, we would like to express our gratitude to the many insurance regulators, professional service advisors and industry colleagues who have supported our efforts and worked with us over the years.

Thank you everyone.

FOREWORD
BY DICK GOFF

Your usual authors typically base their work on decades of experience when describing a field so nuanced as captive insurance. But Michael DiMayo and Kevin Myers are not your usual authors. They came to the captive world, which we like to call ART for alternative risk transfer, within recent years and ART will never be the same.

Mike and Kevin brought a whole new gene pool to ART from their decades of successful experience in sophisticated levels of insurance and financial services. They told me that the light bulb flashed over their heads when they attended a seminar on captives put on by the Delaware Department of Insurance Captive Bureau. Suddenly, they say, the possibilities for bringing Fortune 500-style enterprise risk management to small to mid-size organizations compelled them to learn more.

And learn they did, as they picked the brains of many of us who have worked in the ART world for most of our careers. Their company, Oxford Risk Management Group, collected the wisdom and data that would bring it to prominence as a think tank for our industry.

They brought with them the best characteristics of big business: making customer service a strategic element of the enterprise rather than an afterthought; building teams comprised of specialists with "Best-in-Class" reputations; and working through a stratospherically high level of producers as their national marketing arm.

Customer service gets a whole new level of attention from Mike and Kevin, compared to the usual experience in the field. From the earliest encounters, all their information is presented clearly and concisely in simple language, and all the details are included. "Transparency" is a recently adopted business buzzword but it's the way of life for Mike and Kevin who really do live in a glass house.

Oxford, for example, recently published an executive briefing for their members so that information about the program and how it works can be distributed through member organizations and outside consultants and service providers. The book you are now reading is another example of their zealous insistence on education for all their colleagues, network and other readers.

Mike and Kevin's team building is legendary, having grown from their own team of two that brings complementary back-grounds and talents to their enterprise. In their dealings with clients, consultants, regulators or others they scarcely encounter any position that they haven't researched in advance. With them, there are no surprises on either side of the table.

They have built a specialist infrastructure to serve the needs of their company and their clients. Our own Taft Companies are proud to be part of that in the role of captive manager which you will learn about in Chapter 7. I can attest to the fact that members of Oxford's service provider team come to think of themselves as integral to its mission and culture rather than remaining in the position of outsiders.

What Oxford describes as its "Best-in-Class" team of profes-sional specialists also includes attorneys who live and breathe captive insurance every day, and a leading national actuarial firm that helps keep every case underwritten on an even keel. You'll learn how these professionals help Oxford members avoid dangerous legal and economic pitfalls in Chapter 8.

And Oxford's team of highest-level insurance intermediaries and producers serves to disseminate vital information about its programs and benefits to the many companies and organizations that are still seeking the best enterprise risk management method.

Heck, Mike and Kevin haven't just built a "dream team," they've built an entire ART fantasy league.

Now, you can absorb the best and most concise introduction to captive insurance companies that I've ever read: what they are, how they benefit their owners, how to decide if one is good for you, along with illuminating details of how to create a captive most efficiently and economically while remaining in compliance with all laws and regulations.

That's a big order for a little book, but come to think of it, that's the Oxford way.

*Dick Goff is managing member of The Taft Companies, LLC, a captive insurance management firm at **www.taftcos.com**. He writes the monthly ART Gallery column in The Self-Insurer magazine.*

ABOUT THE AUTHORS

"I am no stranger to working hard. I have done it all my life. As a result I have become accustomed to expecting success in everything I do. Some people call me lucky, but I know better."

- Donald Trump,
Think Big

Michael A. DiMayo, CFP®, CLU, ChFC
Principal, Oxford Risk Management Group;
Founder, The Affluence Group, LLC

Mike's distinction as one of the most successful insurance brokers in the business gained him national notoriety and prestige. According to a lead advanced sales attorney with one major insurance company, "No one can take complex topics and make them clear and easy to understand the way Mike does."

As a graduate of Franklin & Marshall College, Mike enjoyed a prominent career spanning 29 years as the most successful producer in the history of The Hartford Life, until starting his own insurance company, The Affluence Group, LLC in 2008. Mike joined forces with Kevin Myers, CPA, M.S. Taxation, to form Oxford Risk Management Group.

He is a 27-year member of the Society of Financial Service Professionals, a member of the Baltimore Estate Planning Council and has served as keynote speaker for numerous industry and

Oxford Research Group, LLC is a limited liability company formed under the Maryland Limited Liability Company Act with corporate offices located in Sparks, Maryland. Oxford Research Group, LLC provides educational and feasibility services and conducts business entirely from its corporate office located at:

Oxford Research Group, LLC
954 Ridgebrook Road, Suite 120
Sparks, Maryland 21152

The information contained in this book is not intended to provide insurance, tax or legal advice of any kind. Readers are directed to seek professional advice from their own legal, accounting, insurance and investment advisors.

INTRODUCTION

Now that you have a copy of *Discovering Captives*, you would probably like to have an executive summary of what our book on captive insurance companies is all about and how you stand to benefit from reading about them.

Risk management is an important part of every business. If you are the owner of a successful business, your company is likely to have traditional property and casualty policies in place for the business risks that can be readily identified such as workers' compensation, automobile, liability, etc. Those are the easy ones to identify. However, you are likely to also have exposure to enterprise risks for which you have no coverage, yet losses from those risks can result in significant adverse consequences for your company.

- You will learn what those risks are and how a captive can help you to more effectively manage them.

- You will learn how a captive can provide specialized coverage with policy features tailored to meet your specific needs. Your coverage...provided by your own insurance company...on your own terms.

- You will learn how a captive provides financial incentives to generate and capture underwriting profits for you and your business, rather than for a third-party commercial insurer.

- This book provides a step-by-step roadmap detailing the process to follow to reap the rewards of operating your own insurance company.

We start by explaining what a captive insurance company is. We then walk you through everything you need to know to benefit from this exciting tool. And we help you identify and avoid potential obstacles along the way. From start to finish, we promise to tell the whole story and explain each concept from the perspective of successful business owners and key advisors, in plain English.

Ok—let's get started!

CHAPTER ONE

WHAT IS A CAPTIVE?

"The first step in the risk management process is to acknowledge the reality of risk. Denial is a common tactic that substitutes deliberate ignorance for thoughtful planning."

- **Charles Tremper,**
Writer on Risk Management

A captive insurance company (also called a captive) is a property and casualty insurance company established to provide coverage primarily for a parent company. Think of it as a mini GEICO© or State Farm© that a business owner sets up to insure his/her own company. In many cases, the owner of the parent company is also the owner of the captive; however, the arrangement may also be structured so the captive is owned directly by the operating company, another person, entity or trust. The captive insurance company must act as a legitimate business entity and must remain in compliance with all insurance regulatory provisions and Internal Revenue Service (IRS) requirements.

Why would a business owner form his own insurance company? We'll go into that in greater detail in Chapters 2 and 10, but the main reasons boil down to risk management and economics.

First, a captive can be a valuable tool that allows businesses to more effectively manage business risks. Captives often are set up to insure enterprise risk. Enterprise risk is loosely defined as the broad array of risks to which a business is exposed, but for which it is typically not insured, often because such insurance is not available or is too expensive.

> Enterprise risk is different from the typical commercial coverage (workers' compensation, general liability or automobile, for example) that most businesses purchase.

These days, enterprise risk includes all kinds of risks across all sorts of industries and professions. For example, loss of a business license or professional license, adverse financial impact of regulatory or legislative changes, loss of a key vendor or major client, loss of a franchise license or lease, environmental losses, regulatory inspection failure and the list goes on and on.

Consider a physician who may be accused of performing unnecessary surgical procedures. As he prepares his defense, he may face significant reputational damage from members in the community, other physicians, or public advertisements from law firms seeking to identify potential claimants. Additionally, he may suffer a loss of privileges at his hospital or surgical center or even worse, a temporary or permanent loss of medical license or certification. These are risks likely to cause a loss of income for the client, yet most physicians are self-insured for them. A captive insurance company can be implemented to provide coverage for these risks and other self-insured exposures, which may not be available in the traditional commercial marketplace.

Second, captives can help businesses control their insurance costs. By forming a captive insurance company, a business can dramatically lower insurance costs in comparison to premiums paid to a conventional property and casualty insurance company. A business owner can address the company's self-insured risks by paying tax-deductible premiums to its captive insurance company. To the extent the captive generates profit—premiums received less claims payments and expenses—those dollars belong to the owner of the captive.

Let's say you went to a specialty insurer, such as Lloyd's of London, and asked them to build a specialty policy for your company. If you don't have any claims one year, then Lloyd's would get to keep all your profits for that year. An alternative to purchasing a specialty property and casualty insurance policy is to simply establish a sinking fund to accumulate reserves to meet those losses. Allocating balance sheet reserves to a sinking fund is one way to prepare for potential self-insured risks. Your operating company may be prudent to set aside liquidity on its balance sheet but, as we all know, there's no tax deduction for that.

However, payment of an insurance premium for property and casualty coverage is an ordinary and necessary business expense—which is tax-deductible. So the advantage of forming your own captive insurance company is that, if you control expenses and manage claims effectively, instead of a third-party insurance company profiting from all that surplus year to year, your own insurance company gets to capture the profits. If you

The concept of a business forming a wholly-owned insurance company to insure its owner's risks can be traced back to the group of London merchants who lost their assets in the Tooley Street fire in 1861. The concept continued in the 1920's when several corporations with multi-national interests, including British Petroleum, Unilever and Lufthansa, each formed wholly-owned insurance companies.

The late Fred Reiss conceived and marketed the concept of a wholly-owned insurance company, which he called a "captive." Captives have stood the test of time since 1957 when Reiss formed his first captive in Cleveland, Ohio, for the Youngstown Sheet and Tube Company. Most Fortune 1000 companies have their own captives. Here are a few examples:

New York Times Company –
Midtown Insurance Company

Allstate Insurance Company –
formerly a captive owned by Sears & Roebuck Company

General Mills –
Gold Medal Insurance Company

Prudential Insurance Company –
New Jersey Captive Insurance Company

Thousands of small companies have also set up captive insurance companies and, until recently, the overwhelming majority of captive insurance companies were created in offshore jurisdictions.

What has recently changed is the ability for business owners to form a conservative, highly regulated captive insurance structure within the U.S. at a reasonable cost. Numerous states have introduced revised captive insurance laws, allowing formation of these entities at cost-effective levels.

Historically, businesses interested in forming their own captives had to hire an actuary, a captive manager, risk manager, attorney—a whole team of licensed professionals that, domestically, was cost-prohibitive for many small to medium sized businesses. Unless you had a minimum of $1 million in paid annual premiums, it didn't make sense. This is no longer the case. Small to mid-size businesses can consider as little as $50,000 in annual premium payments by working with a seasoned captive advisory firm offering turn-key implementation services.

There are no firm rules regarding the minimum amount of gross revenue a company should have in order to benefit from forming a captive insurance company nor is there a minimum amount of annual insurance premiums a company should be prepared to pay before it considers forming a captive. In order to successfully implement and manage the captive insurance company, there are a number of professionals who must be engaged to help develop, implement and provide administrative management for the company. That's where a company like Oxford Risk Management Group comes in. But we'll get into that in more detail in Chapters 7 and 9. Right now, let's move on to find out—Why Form a Captive?

CHAPTER TWO

WHY FORM A CAPTIVE?

"If you don't invest in risk management,
it doesn't matter what business
you're in, it's a risky business."

- Gary D. Cohn,
President and COO, Goldman Sachs

There are many potential advantages to forming a captive insurance company. As we discussed in the last chapter, captives are created for both risk management and economic purposes. By establishing your own insurance company, you potentially create a brand new profit center instead of paying costly premiums to a conventional property and casualty insurance company.

The premiums paid by your business to the captive are tax-deductible as an ordinary and necessary business expense, just as they would be treated had they been made to a traditional insurance company.

But here's where it gets even better: the underwriting profits from premiums that your captive collects are tax-free. Internal Revenue Code Section 831(b) allows certain captive insurance companies to be taxed only on their investment income. They do not pay income tax on the premiums they collect, nor on the earned underwriting profits, provided that net or direct premiums do not exceed $1.2 million per year. Further, the captive may build surplus from underwriting profits free from income tax.

> **Profits result from favorable management of expenses and claims each year, while surplus represents the accumulation of profits over time.**

Take a moment to think about the enormous expenses a conventional insurance company faces as part of its daily operations: payroll, employee health insurance and pension, rent, staffing for the legal, actuarial and claims departments, sales team expenses and commissions, advertising and profit margin, just to name a few. A huge percentage of the premiums you pay for a property and casualty insurance policy is eaten up by these expenses.

When you purchase your insurance coverage from a captive insurance company, your premiums aren't helping to pay a conventional insurance company's costs for overhead, marketing, agent commissions, sales incentive conventions, advertising, profits, etc. In fact, you will be motivated to control operational costs and claims,

---

Businesses from many industries can benefit from a captive insurance company. The list is virtually limitless, including:

Accounting Firms, Agriculture, Automobile, Banking, Consulting, Construction, Distribution, Entertainment, Environmental, Farming, Family Office, Financial Services, Franchise, Government Contracting, Health Care, Investment Advisory, Legal, Medical, Manufacturing, Pro Athletes, Sales, Professional Service Firms, Real Estate, Restaurants, Technology, Transportation

and you may gain significant savings in the form of underwriting profits. Your captive insurance company will probably not advertise during the Super Bowl and is unlikely to create a corporate mascot or cartoon character to represent it. The owner of the captive will retain the profits generated. Over the years, profits and surplus may accumulate to sizeable amounts and may be distributed to the owner(s) of the captive company, under favorable income tax rates as either dividends or long-term capital gains.

Let's look at an example. Suppose your business pays $1 million in premium to a captive insurance company every year. Assume further that your combined federal and state income tax rate is 45%. Your business would deduct $1 million from its taxable income, saving you $450,000 each year. Furthermore, that $1 million would be received free of income tax each year inside your captive insurance company. In addition to receiving substantial risk management benefits, you would lower your income tax bill considerably, pay far less in taxes and have more money in the bank as a result. When you no longer need the insurance benefits a captive insurance company provides, the owner of the captive can take a dividend distribution from the company or can elect to liquidate the captive subject to historically favorable capital gains rates.

A captive insurance company can also provide protection against risks that prove to be too costly in commercial markets or may be generally unavailable. The inability to obtain specialized types of coverage from commercial third-party insurers is another reason why clients may choose to establish a captive. For example, your company may be subject to economic loss due to governmental regulatory or legislative changes. While it would make a lot of sense for you to purchase coverage for protection from these risks, you may find that this type of policy is simply unavailable. Your captive insurance company is better equipped to offer specialized coverage, tailored specifically to your unique business needs.

It's important to understand that while a captive can be utilized to replace your existing insurance coverage, this may not always be the case. Coverage issued by the captive, such as deductible reimbursement, doesn't have to take the place of existing coverage, especially when your current policies provide coverage against the types of risks which may result in catastrophic losses. Your captive can help you build a policy engineered to supplement these traditional lines of coverage you already enjoy.

In most cases, to the extent existing property and casualty coverage is reasonably priced, the most attractive option may be to retain existing policies for your traditional coverage, supplementing it by addressing self-insured risks with your own captive insurance company.

Policy features, coverage and limits can be drafted to meet specific enterprise exposures. This allows for various risk management advantages, including:

1. **Greater Control over Claims**

    You control the claims review process and have direct control over how claims are handled, delivering improved service to the insured.

2. **Increased Coverage**

    Your captive policy can provide coverage for exposures that may be unavailable from traditional, third-party property and casualty carriers.

3. Increased Capacity

Your captive policy can provide coverage at limits that may be unavailable from traditional, third-party property and casualty carriers.

4. Underwriting Flexibility

Policy features can be customized to meet your specific needs. You get to decide on limitations and/or exclusions, subject to insurance regulatory approval.

5. Access Reinsurance Market

Your captive insurance company has direct access to the reinsurance marketplace.

6. Incentive for Loss Control

Underwriting profits belong to the owner of the captive insurance company, providing a powerful incentive to implement loss control measures and reduce claims experience.

7. Reduced Insurance Costs

Your captive insurance company can help you reduce the cost of your coverage, providing valuable savings to the insured.

Ten years ago if you asked an automobile dealer to insure for loss of franchise risk, he would not even bother to speak about it as a relevant exposure. It was simply unheard of in the auto dealer industry. Just in the last five years, hundreds of Chrysler and General Motors franchises have not been renewed and brands discontinued. The automobile dealers who depended on new auto sales revenue, repairs and warranty revenue, and rental income for their business to succeed were suddenly out of business. We now have seen auto dealers who have set aside captive premium dollars to insure for a potential risk for loss of franchise.

8. **Capture Underwriting Profit**

   Underwriting profits belong to the owner of the captive insurance company, rather than a third-party commercial property and casualty insurance carrier.

9. **Pricing Stability**

   You can anticipate stable pricing, thanks to sound loss control methods and reduced claims experience.

10. **Improved Claims Review and Processing**

    You can establish best practices and implementation for enhanced claims processing, electronic claims payments, etc.

11. **Purchase Based on Need**

    You get to design your policy to include coverage you actually need, rather than pre-established template policy forms, and you can update coverage as your needs change.

12. **Tax Benefits**

    Underwriting profits are tax-exempt under IRC 831(b) and are only taxed when distributed to the owner of the captive.

13. **Investment Income**

    Your captive gets to invest its reserves and surplus, allowing investment income to benefit you rather than the third-party commercial insurance carrier.

14. **Additional Profit Center**

    Your captive is a bona fide property and casualty insurance company, operating with the business purpose of managing risk and generating underwriting profit. After payment of expenses and claims, profits belong to you.

As you can see, there are many valuable risk management benefits from forming a captive insurance company. There are also significant tax benefits including, that premiums paid by your business to the captive are tax-deductible as an ordinary and necessary business expense. Your captive does not pay income tax on the premium it collects, providing those premiums do not exceed $1.2 million per year. Further, the captive may retain surplus from underwriting profits free from income tax. The captive only pays current tax on investment earnings.

CHAPTER THREE

CAPTIVE MYTHS AND MISCONCEPTIONS

"The great enemy of truth is very often not the lie—deliberate, contrived and dishonest—but the myths—persistent, persuasive, and unrealistic. Too often we enjoy the comfort of opinion without the discomfort of thought."

- **John F. Kennedy,**
35th President

OK, we've talked about what a captive insurance company is and also identified reasons why you might consider forming one for yourself. Hopefully, those reasons made sense and you were able to relate to some of them.

Over the years, our advisory group has identified numerous beliefs and notions about captive insurance companies that can fit the general heading of "myths and misconceptions." Like anything in life, whether folklore, celebrity or even financial products, you will find that there are myths and misconceptions regarding just about any topic. These beliefs and notions share a common lack of factual basis. Let's take a look at some of these myths about captives, try to sort out fact from fiction, and dispel the misinformation so that you are in the best position to properly evaluate them and form your own opinions:

Myth 1: "Captives are a new concept."

Reality: This is certainly not true. Captive insurance planning has been around in its most primitive form since the late 1800's and domestically since the mid 1950's. The only thing that is relatively new today is that top quality domestic captive domiciles continue to update their statutes, allowing for more cost-efficient implementation and management. Captive programs offered by our group have been formed to maximize the advantages of beneficial laws in attractive jurisdictions both domestic and international. Captive arrangements are now affordable and user-friendly for the small to mid-size business owner.

Myth 2: "Captives are too expensive for my small business. I heard that they are only for Fortune 1000 type companies."

Reality: Not true. Captive insurance companies are, in fact, utilized by the majority of large companies in corporate America and abroad. Large captives can be very complex and indeed costly to implement and maintain. However, captives are no longer cost prohibitive for the small to mid-size business owner. Modern captive statutes and regulatory requirements now make it cost-efficient for companies to utilize captive programs and enjoy the resulting risk management benefits for as little as $50,000 in annual paid-in premium!

Myth 3: "I heard that captives only insure liability type coverage, but my annual premium expenditure is too small to warrant a captive."

Reality: While liability and other lines of coverage can be incorporated into attractive captive arrangements, there are numerous additional types of coverage you may also underwrite. Available coverage and premiums for your captive should coordinate with your existing property and casualty policies but have little to do with your current premium expenditures.

Myth 4: "I've been told if something sounds too good to be true it probably is."

Reality: OK, we'll agree with that sentiment, but not in the context of a legitimate captive insurance company. Your captive will be a meaningful risk management tool, providing real coverage at appropriate premium levels. Your captive will be subject to review and ongoing supervision by the insurance regulators in your chosen domicile. As noted earlier, many captives have been in existence for a very long time. The good news is that captive pricing is within reach for most companies today.

Myth 5: "Captives are listed transactions."

Reality: This bit of folklore carries on today as a testament to the notion that you can't believe everything you read on the Internet. Not long ago, this inaccurate myth was posted on a website, resulting in a great deal of criticism for the author. Certain types of captive arrangements, known as producer-owned reinsurance companies, used to be deemed listed transactions. They were delisted in IRS Notice 2004-65.

Myth 6: "This is a tax shelter and not real insurance."

Reality: Really? Captive insurance arrangements do provide valuable risk management advantages and enjoy income tax benefits, as insurance companies do. However, let's not lose sight of the fact that they are heavily scrutinized and regulated by diligent insurance departments within the United States and internationally. Insurance companies of all sizes (from your captive insurance company to large commercial carriers) are evaluated for appropriate risk-sharing and risk-distribution, valid coverage, liquidity and solvency standards, and appropriate premiums. This is as real as it gets!

Myth 7: "The IRS is looking into captives and is going to be coming down on them."

Reality: Since its establishment in 1862, the IRS is responsible for the collection of taxes and enforcement of our country's tax code. The IRS has issued numerous rulings and related guidance defining the rules of the road for captive insurance arrangements. It is reasonable to expect them to monitor taxpayer compliance with these rules. There are sure to be folks out there who will stretch the limits and push the envelope with any given arrangement, and the captive industry is no exception. It is important to utilize a conservative, compliant structure and partner with professional advisors who understand the rules and stick to them.

Myth 8: "You must pay a large fee just to see if a captive works for your company."

Reality: There are many groups out there that will charge an upfront fee generally ranging from $5,000-$20,000 just to let you know if you can benefit from a captive insurance company.

However, this is not always the case and you should locate a professional firm that will conduct the initial feasibility analysis at little to no cost.

Myth 9: "Captives take a very long time to create—I do not have that kind of time, nor do I want the headache."

Reality: Modern statutes have made the captive formation process more user-friendly. There are professional captive advisory firms out there that can manage your implementation in a turn-key, efficient and stress-free manner. It is certainly possible to finalize your new captive insurance company on a fast track basis if you are a motivated and responsive participant in the process.

Myth 10: "Captives are a way to buy tax-deductible life insurance."

Reality: This myth is not only incorrect but can lead to undesired results. First and foremost, captive insurance companies, as discussed in this book, are only formed for risk management purposes and offer property and casualty coverage. While appropriately designed life insurance policies MAY possess investment attributes consistent with your captive investment plan, you should proceed with caution. More about this topic in Chapter 5 on business and investment plans.

Myth 11: "I do not have the time or knowledge to run my own insurance company."

Reality: Few clients do, as they already have full-time jobs and responsibilities. While you may be the owner of the captive and paying the premium from your operating company, you will not be running the day-to-day operations. For example, our firm brings together a team of licensed service providers in many fields to form, manage, and oversee your captive from start to finish.

In your selection process, it would be wise to select a team that can help you implement a captive on a turn-key basis, and also remain at your service for any administrative issues that may develop after your captive is up and running.

In Chapter 7 we'll be talking about your professional advisory team in greater detail. For once, you will be in control of the insurance company, enjoying all of the resulting benefits, as your expert team runs the daily operations of your captive insurance company.

Myth 12: "I cannot direct the money inside my captive investment plan."

Reality: You get to work with the professional investment advisor of your choice, in management of the captive insurance company assets. Yes, your captive assets must be invested within the general parameters of an investment plan filed with the insurance regulators. Your captive investment plan should direct investments in an appropriate and prudent manner, as allowed by the domicile regulating the captive. If directing the assets inside your captive is important, then you need to choose a structure that allows you to do so, provided you stay within approved investment plan guidelines.

While there are likely many more myths and misconceptions regarding captives, we hope that this addresses some of the typical nonsense floating about the marketplace. If you do hear something you may think is a myth or misconception and would like clarity on the subject, be sure to consult with your captive advisory firm to get the facts.

CHAPTER FOUR

DOMICILE SELECTION: INTERNATIONAL OR DOMESTIC?

"Location is the key to most businesses, and the entrepreneurs typically build their reputation at a particular spot."

- **Phyllis Schlafly,**
Activist and Author

do·mi·cile *noun*
1. the place where a person has his/her permanent principal home to which he/she returns or intends to return.
2. a business has its domicile in the state where its headquarters is located.

It's a pretty safe bet that at one time or another, we've all heard the following advice—when it comes to real estate what matters most is location, location, location. When it comes to selecting a home for your captive insurance company, domicile selection is one of the most important factors to consider. Historically, the vast majority of new captive insurance companies created worldwide have been established in international domiciles, or "offshore."

This is largely because Fred Reiss, creator of the first captive insurance company for Youngstown Sheet and Tube Company in the 1950's, also created the first "captive management company"—International Risk Management Limited—in Bermuda in 1962.

Bermuda has since become world renowned for its captive insurance industry, enjoying the greatest number of licensed captives in the world although many other countries also host vibrant captive insurance markets. In fact, not that long ago, if you wanted to form a captive you were almost forced to go offshore to places such as Bermuda, Cayman Islands, British Virgin Islands, or Guernsey, to name a few. There are a variety of reasons for this including solid laws governing captives, top-flight regulators, and experienced captive management, actuarial and legal professionals to service the industry. Additionally, captive arrangements in international domiciles can be accomplished with very attractive cost and capital requirements, allowing for cost-effective implementation for the smallest of captives. In general, implementation and ongoing management costs for the majority of domestic platforms simply weren't cost-effective for a client unless their program generated $1 million or more in annual premium payments.

In the 1970's, the first U.S. special law to encourage captive formation was passed in Colorado, followed by Tennessee, then Vermont. Vermont became one of the first states in the U.S. to both enact favorable captive legislation and also attract a significant number of captives, establishing it as a business-friendly climate for companies forming captives. Over the past decade, there has been a growing number of U.S. jurisdictions allowing captive formation. In the past several years, the number of domestic captives has increased at a rapid pace as an increasing number of states have passed captive legislation and/or modified existing legislation to make them more attractive to prospective businesses.

Today, more than half of U.S. jurisdictions have captive licensing laws. Vermont, which began licensing captives in 1981, is the largest onshore captive domicile, and other states have been taking steps to become more attractive. Their efforts are beginning to gain ground. Utah, Kentucky, Montana and Delaware, for example, have each experienced double-digit growth in business between 2010 and 2011, according to recent domestic industry reports.

"I've always been in the right place and time. Of course, I steered myself there."

- **Bob Hope,**
Comedian

In fact, 2011 was the first year in which more captives were formed in domestic jurisdictions than were formed within international domiciles. Many U.S. states have enacted business-friendly captive insurance laws that permit you to do everything from here in the U.S., in a cost-effective manner. Not only do more than half of U.S. jurisdictions have captive licensing laws, but also many have either approved new captive legislation or amended their existing captive statutes. This makes it possible for the business owner to enjoy many of the benefits previously associated only with international domiciles.

The recent growth spurt among captives opting to domicile domestically can be attributed to lower implementation costs and hurdles, manageable capitalization requirements and state legislators willing to provide increasingly flexible provisions in their captive statutes.

What factors should be considered in selecting the domicile for a captive insurer? [1]

1. Lines of insurance the domicile permits a captive to write,

2. Accessibility to regulators and governmental officials that act on the legislation and regulations that impact captives,

3. Legislative and regulatory philosophy, commitment, and appreciation of captive insurance companies,

4. Supporting infrastructure in the domicile (i.e. captive managers, third-party administrators, legal counsel, investment managers and consultants, banking services, telecommunications, captive insurance association, availability of insurance professionals if the captive is to be staffed in-house, and access to air transportation),

5. Regulatory reporting requirements,

6. Requirements of records and files that must be maintained in the domicile and therefore duplicated if captive administrative offices are located elsewhere,

7. Flexibility for a captive to set its rates without prior approval of the domicile regulator,

8. Investment restrictions,

9. Premium taxes,

10. Requirements for meetings of the board of directors of the captive,

11. How the domicile charges expenses for regulatory examinations and timeliness of regulatory exam reports, and

12. The adequacy and competency of staff in the domicile regulatory agency.

There are many excellent jurisdictions to consider, including domestic and international domiciles. While many of the leading domiciles have favorable laws, no one jurisdiction offers the best solution for every client and every captive. Items to consider when selecting the most appropriate domicile will include: taxation, regulation, infrastructure, compliance, investment objectives and overall perception of the domicile and related structures. It is also important to analyze first year implementation and ongoing management costs to remain compliant in the jurisdiction you select for your captive insurance company.

In addition to the domicile attributes noted above, you may be required to travel to the jurisdiction to perform any implementation activities and physically form the captive insurance company. Additionally, most jurisdictions require the captive to have at least one meeting per year within the jurisdiction, along with a local registered agent and physical address. These requirements can often be handled by the captive management and legal service providers.

Working with an expert team of advisors to set up your captive is crucial because they have the regulatory relationships, experience and knowledge to assist in the selection of the most appropriate domicile to generate the most favorable risk management, compliance, profitability, tax and legal results.

---

1. Captive.com, "Twelve Helpful Tips on Selecting a Domicile"

Expert, independent advisors like the ones we employ at our company, Oxford Risk Management Group, can also help to evaluate the effectiveness of existing captive insurance structures for business owners contemplating redomiciling their captive. Given the current climate of increased scrutiny of international business arrangements, many clients have elected to explore domestic captive formation for enhanced peace of mind. Alternatively, many clients have elected to structure their captive insurance company in conformity with U.S. regulatory requirements in a more cost-efficient international domicile.

"Clients do not expect the infrastructure
to be any less reliable just because the service
is being delivered from an offshore location."

- Sanjay Kumar,
Retired Chairman, Computer Associates

If you have heard of captive insurance, you might have some misguided perceptions about it. After all, offshore investments are a hotly debated topic in our current political and economic climate. Misguided perceptions about international finance, banking and insurance have led some advisors to steer their clients away from international domiciles. You should keep an open mind when evaluating domestic and international domiciles, in part because offshore jurisdictions continue to improve their captive laws, just as domestic legislatures and regulators continually refine and improve theirs.

For example:

- Earlier this year, Cayman proposed a new form of incorporated cell company legislation that would amend the Cayman Islands Insurance Law so as to allow insurers formed as segregated portfolio companies (SPCs) to enjoy the same benefits as incorporated cell companies in other jurisdictions.

- The first protected cell companies (PCCs) originated in Guernsey with the passing of the Protected Cell Companies Ordinance in 1997. Ever since, these effective self-insurance vehicles have popped up in other offshore jurisdictions including the Cayman Islands, Bermuda and Mauritius. However, as the first domicile to establish PCCs, it can be said that Guernsey has a historical advantage over other offshore domiciles.

- Soon the Financial Services Authority (FSA) will cease to exist as the United Kingdom's sole financial services regulator. In its place will be three new regulatory entities: the Financial Policy Committee (FPC), the Prudential Regulation Authority (PRA) and the Financial Conduct Authority (FCA). The so-called "twin peaks" model, which is to be adopted, referring to the split between conduct and prudential regulation, will create two new supervisors for regulated firms.

There are many highly qualified regulators in a variety of quality domiciles to consider, allowing your captive to be designed to meet your specific risk management and financial objectives.

CHAPTER FIVE

BUSINESS AND INVESTMENT PLAN DESIGN

"By failing to prepare, you are preparing to fail."

- **Benjamin Franklin,**
Founding Father and Statesman

A well conceived business plan is an important component of any successful business. A sound business plan lays the foundation for captive operations and profitability expectations, and provides a yardstick against which yearly results can be measured and evaluated. Most captive domiciles require a business plan and will thoroughly review it before approving a captive insurance company.

The captive management firm will help you create a business plan, detailing the anticipated operation of your captive company. This plan will be shared with the insurance regulatory team in your chosen domicile as

> The business plan is often a collaborative effort between the captive management firm, the actuarial consultant and legal counsel. To ensure ongoing compliance, any changes in the business plan must be filed with and approved by the insurance regulatory team in your domicile.

CHAPTER SIX

CAPTIVE COSTS, FEES AND THE IMPORTANCE OF TRANSPARENCY

"The most important thing in communication is to hear what isn't being said."

- **Peter F. Drucker,**
Management Consultant, Educator and Author

While there are many important aspects to consider when forming your captive insurance company, two questions come to the forefront of every client's mind: "What is it going to cost to set up and what are the ongoing expenses to be paid?" Cost is a major factor (and sometimes hurdle) when establishing your captive and should be evaluated very closely to make sure you are selecting the structure that is right for you.

With numerous captive providers and structures in the marketplace it makes sense to compare costs the same way one may shop around to purchase an automobile. However, when shopping around it is important to pay attention to the fact that while structures may seem to be the same from initial discussions, they may be vastly different from one another. This is why it is really

2. **What is the cost for the feasibility study?**

Many captive providers charge a non-refundable fee to see if the captive is even a fit for the client. In the event you decide to move forward with your captive, a comprehensive feasibility study will ultimately be required as part of the implementation process—see Chapter 9. However, there should not be an upfront charge to determine if a captive may be a good fit.

3. **Are there any fees associated with the use of the risk pool?**

A bona fide captive insurance company needs to satisfy IRS requirements for sharing risk with others. In order to satisfy this requirement, some captive providers charge an annual fee to use their risk pool either in the form of a flat fee or percentage of premium. Risk pools can be built solely for risk-sharing and risk-distribution, not to generate additional profit.

"The only image we've ever had is what we really are. We never cover up anything."

\- Angus Young,
Lead Guitarist, AC/DC

4. **Are there any asset-based charges and if so how are they calculated?**

Some providers charge asset-based fees on top of asset management fees. These should be disclosed, including: the fee schedule, the portion of captive assets subject to them and when fees are levied from the captive's account.

5. **Are there any associated fees or cost for the purchase of reinsurance and if so who are these paid to and who is providing that reinsurance?**

   Some structures require the purchase of reinsurance for the coverage being provided. Sometimes this coverage is paid to valid reinsurance carriers and sometimes it is paid to an additional profit center being run by the captive provider.

6. **Is the annual audit cost included in the annual fees or is that an additional expense?**

   Annual audit fees can typically cost $7,000-$13,000 per year and should be disclosed or included in the costs quoted.

7. **Are there any additional fees during the renewal process for the annual review of premiums?**

   The renewal process should be part of the annual fees and fully disclosed to the client.

8. **Are there any termination fees when I shut down my captive?**

   When shutting down the captive, some providers charge a termination fee that could be a flat fee or based on a percentage of total captive assets at the time (usually with a minimum charge).

9. **Does the cost quoted include ALL of the required licensed service providers who run the captive?**

   These include the captive manager, legal counsel, tax counsel, actuarial and audit firms.

10. Does the annual cost include the filing of the annual tax return?

The annual tax return for the captive is generally completed and filed by your own professional tax advisor, at your own expense.

11. Does the fee schedule include filing fees both during application and any associated annual filing fees?

Domicile-specific fees can vary greatly and are generally not included in estimates for implementation and management of your captive. There are usually filing, application and other user fees assessed by the domicile, in addition to premium tax liability based on paid premiums.

12. Does the investment return for captive assets invested or allocated to the risk pool belong to my captive 100% or does the captive provider retain a portion of that?

Allocation of the captive assets and investment income generated can have a material impact on the total investment return. You should verify the extent to which investment returns are retained by the structure, rather than allocated to your captive investment portfolio.

13. What are the statutory capital requirements for the type of captive you are forming?

Captives are typically required to establish and maintain certain minimum levels of capital and surplus, which can vary by domicile and type of captive. Though capital is not an expense, you should account for capital requirements in considering the cost of forming a captive.

14. Are there ANY OTHER fees that may be charged that are not listed on the fee schedule?

As you can see, there are many questions that need to be asked regarding a captive fee schedule and the costs could add up. While at first glance a fee schedule may seem competitive, it should be evaluated very closely. This chapter emphasizes the importance of an easy to understand and explainable fee schedule. If the fee schedule is truly "turn-key" then the above should be able to be explained in five minutes or less.

CHAPTER SEVEN

SUCCESSFUL CAPTIVE IMPLEMENTATION AND MANAGEMENT

"The best executive is the one who has sense enough to pick good men to do what he wants done and self-restraint enough to keep from meddling with them while they do it."

- Theodore Roosevelt,
26th President

If you want your captive to work, it has to be done right. The following roadmap to successful implementation and management of your captive details the process and steps to take, but your captive advisory team will handle these steps for you without complexity on your part.

After you have reviewed your options and made a decision on the domicile that best fits your particular risk management and financial objectives, you must develop a plan on how to manage your captive.

Because few companies are in the business of insurance themselves, most captives will need to retain the services of a qualified captive management firm to manage the day-to-day operations of the captive for them. In most domiciles, you will be required to select a captive management firm from a list of approved companies, who have been pre-screened by the insurance regulators.

The key purpose of insurance regulation is to protect policyholders first and foremost, as well as investors and other stakeholders. Like traditional insurance companies, captives are regulated by the domicile in which their headquarters are located. However, a captive is different from a commercial insurance company in that it just serves its parent company. Therefore, captives are regulated differently than traditional insurance companies that serve the public.

It is essential that the captive management firm you select has extensive experience in this space. They should also have a good rapport and working relationship with the insurance regulatory team in the domicile you have selected. In our experience, without question, clients benefit from an approach that delivers independent, Best-in-Class experts to guide them through each and every aspect of their captive insurance company structure.

Let's take a look at the various professionals who will be retained to ensure that your captive is implemented and managed in a manner consistent with the rules of the road:

The **Captive Manager** is in many ways the quarterback of your captive advisory team. The manager functions as an extension of the insurance regulators, and is your first source of contact for questions regarding the day-to-day operations of your captive insurance company.

It is vital for your captive insurance company to adhere to the business and investment plans it has filed with the insurance regulators, and working with the insurance regulatory team is an important responsibility of every captive manager. The manager will provide guidance and take responsibility for handling your captive's daily business activities. If the captive manager observes that your captive is not following prudent practices in any critical area—underwriting risk, investment plan decisions, processing claims or other important operations—the manager will suggest steps to remedy the situation. If the captive fails to take action and fails to bring the structure back into compliance, it is the manager's duty to bring this situation to the attention of the insurance department regulators.

It is not unusual for insurance regulators to undergo personnel changes over time, and therefore the expectations of the domicile may change. It is critical that your captive manager maintains a solid working relationship with the regulatory team and remains in touch with evolving management requirements.

The captive manager also has potential responsibility for a variety of other tasks, including:

- Issuing policies
- Processing endorsements and changes
- Premium billing and collection
- Providing risk management services and review
- Opening and overseeing investment accounts
- Claims review and processing
- Maintenance of captive books and records
- Working with auditors and examiners
- Coordinating the activities of legal counsel, actuary and independent auditor
- Acting as liaison with the insurance regulatory professionals

Our lead captive management partners are highly regarded as among the industry's most respected professionals, providing personal, customized services to the alternative risk transfer arena. Your captive management and consulting groups should have extensive expertise in the design and management of innovative value-added captive products and programs. Since 1968, our lead captive manager has held numerous industry leadership positions, having developed extensive experience with captives, insurance companies and reinsurance companies in numerous domiciles around the world.

The selection of **Legal Counsel** is a critical decision for your captive. Once you have selected legal counsel, he or she will be an important member of your captive advisory team. They will assist you in all aspects of the implementation and operation of your captive insurance company. They will also provide advice and assistance with domicile and ownership structure options, formation, licensing, compliance with statutory and regulatory requirements, maintenance of books and records, and representation before the regulatory authorities.

"Why should I clutter my mind with general information when I have men around me who can supply any knowledge I need ? "

- Henry Ford,
American Industrialist

We align our clients with legal counsel who have extensive experience in compliance and regulatory matters, and who maintain strong working relationships with domestic state insurance department regulators as well as financial and monetary authorities in international domiciles. They generally also serve as counsel to all segments of the traditional and alternative risk insurance industries. Our organization strives to engage regulatory attorneys who have assisted in drafting and managing the passage of insurance legislation and have helped to rewrite the law in the jurisdiction you plan to utilize as your captive domicile.

The regulatory attorneys you select should be at the top of their game. Our attorneys are frequently invited to speak at conferences, symposiums, and industry and association meetings throughout the world. Our lead domestic regulatory attorney focuses on the formation, regulation and governance of captive insurance companies. He is a founder and director of the Delaware Captive Insurance Association. He chaired and continues to serve on the committee that drafted Delaware's updated captive insurance statute in 2005. He is active in captive insurance industry associations and frequently speaks on captive insurance topics.

CHAPTER EIGHT

POTENTIAL PITFALLS
TO AVOID

"Summing up, it is clear the future holds great opportunities. It also holds pitfalls. The trick will be to avoid the pitfalls, seize the opportunities, and get back home by six o'clock."

- **Woody Allen,**
American Director, Actor and Comedian

We've talked about many of the things that a captive can help you accomplish but at this point you're probably thinking—what can go wrong? It's safe to say that any good concept improperly executed can generate adverse results. What are the potential problems you need to be aware of and how can you avoid them?

Before we identify possible pitfalls, let's begin the process by restating the obvious. It is crucial that your captive insurance company be structured and managed as a bona fide property and casualty insurance company, providing true risk for appropriate premium levels. You need to follow the rules; it is important to conduct your insurance business according to all of the relevant domicile regulatory rules and IRS guidance and requirements if you want a structure that will deliver predictable results.

The IRS has frequently stated that an insurance contract must fall within the "commonly accepted sense of insurance," yet there is no clear-cut definition to follow. Should your captive insurance arrangement be reviewed upon audit, it is a sure bet that the policies will be reviewed to ascertain if they meet this standard, based upon a number of factual determinations (additional details available in Appendix A). The captive manager and consulting actuary should be of the highest caliber in order to assist in appropriate policy design and pricing. Our firm also retains expert income tax guidance from one of the most respected accounting firms in the country, with considerable experience handling audits, and nationally recognized law firms with significant pedigrees in captive tax law. Experience really does matter!

It is essential that your captive insurance company be organized and operated for bona fide business purposes and demonstrate both risk-shifting and risk-distribution in order for the arrangement to meet the requirements to qualify as insurance in the eyes of the IRS. You should understand that there are areas in which the IRS guidance is clear, yet court decisions have provided more liberal treatment. While many captive management firms believe it to be unnecessary to meet all regulations, more conservative captive plans are designed to comply with each and every bit of IRS guidance.

We constantly have discussions with prospective clients who have been pitched a captive as a tax shelter with no business purpose being considered.

Some of the gimmicks and things to avoid are the following:

- ### Not Following the "Safe Harbor" Guidelines

  Revenue rulings 2002-89 and 2002-90 provide "safe harbor" determinations for risk-distribution if a captive has more than 50% unrelated business risk or a sufficient number of brother-sister related risk. Some courts have suggested lesser risk distributions are sufficient, but the revenue rulings provide certainty. This guides the captive implementation and regulatory team throughout the process, enabling the experts to design a compliant captive insurance company. Through the application of "safe harbor" Revenue Rulings the business owner has a clear path for captive design with predictable tax results.

- ### No Real Shifting of Risk

  The two critical elements of insurance for tax purposes are risk-distribution and risk-shifting. In addition to risk-distribution achieved by following the "safe harbor" revenue rulings, a captive program must achieve risk-shifting, which means shifting the burden of a loss from the insured to the insurer. Risk-shifting is generally achieved when a captive is sufficiently funded by capital and premium, and bears an acceptable chance of loss. Some policy limits and risk pooling vehicles are designed to preclude any real chance of loss and could fail the risk-shifting test.

- ### Loan-Back Provisions

  This is one of our favorites. It is possible to design a captive arrangement which allows the insured to pay its premium to the captive insurance company for property and casualty insurance, and then miraculously receives most of the money a few days or weeks later in the form of a loan. Is this how insurance companies conduct business? Certainly, this "feature" really begs the question—if you are running a legitimate property and casualty company, how can you pay claims if you have no assets in reserve to do so? Did the client implement the captive to manage risk or to attempt to dodge taxes? If you run across a promoter pitching the concept of a loan-back you should head for the hills.

▪ Investment Plans that Don't Make Sense

It is important for the captive to maintain appropriate liquid reserves in order to meet potential claims liabilities. If you are going to operate a legitimate business, it simply makes sense to maintain a reasonable amount of cash in the bank and other liquid assets so that your captive can pay the bills when they are due. Therefore, captive insurance company investment portfolios tend to be conservative and provide significant liquidity. Investing the captive reserves in a beach front property or putting all of the captive premium into a whole life insurance policy with little to no cash value are some of the ways a captive's investment plan can be abused and should be avoided.

▪ Insuring "Bogus" Risks

A captive insurance company can provide protection against risks that prove to be too costly in commercial markets or may be generally unavailable. The inability to obtain specialized types of coverage from commercial third-party insurers is another reason why clients may choose to establish a captive insurance company. Paying $1 million in premium for terrorism coverage when your business is in Peoria, Illinois, or ransom coverage when your employees really don't face such risk doesn't seem to make sense. Do the insurance policies issued by your captive resemble real insurance? If not, why would you purchase it? Remember, just because a regulator in a particular domicile approves a particular policy, it does not automatically follow that the IRS will agree that the captive is providing "insurance in the traditional sense."

- ### Paying a "Bloated" Premium for Coverage

  Let's face it, if your only objective is to generate the biggest tax deduction you can, why not simply inflate the premium to unrealistically high levels, and then shop around until you eventually find a domicile that will approve your design? As an insurance company, a legitimate captive needs to engage the services of a consulting actuary to promulgate insurance rates. The premiums charged by your captive need to be realistic, and similar to rates which would be charged by other insurance companies assuming an arms-length transaction. If your captive charges you an inflated premium based on unrealistic rates, you run the risk of jeopardizing the entire structure.

- ### Treating the Captive Surplus as a Personal Checkbook

  Wouldn't it be nice if you could set up a captive and an ATM card came along with it? That you could simply swipe your card and have personal access whenever you wanted it? Think back to our earlier discussions about managing your captive as a legitimate insurance company, with its own separate assets and arms-length transactions. It is a regulated insurance company and therefore any type of distribution should have prior approval by the insurance regulators.

Case in Point

This is where things can get complicated. For example, we were once asked to review a captive design where a client paid $500,000 premium to their captive insurance company and the reserves were allocated 100% to a life insurance policy with virtually zero cash surrender value in year one. How can the captive pay its bills or claims if there is no cash available to do so? What was the motivation for setting up the captive in the first place? It sure does not seem that the client was setting up its captive with a valid business purpose in mind, and may have done so for the wrong reasons.

Once your captive insurance company is established, an organization should set aside a reasonable amount of time before taking distributions, dividends, or loans from the captive. The key word here is reasonable. Ideally, you should operate your captive insurance company for 7 to 10 years, if possible, before taking money out of it. Clients considering implementing a captive should not have the mindset of pulling all of the profits out each year. Your captive is a legitimate risk management tool, not a tax shelter. A history of paying captive premiums with subsequent annual distributions after each 12 months may not be a wise fact pattern.

- ## Implementing a Captive to Obtain Tax-Deductible Life Insurance

Some people seem to think that premiums for life insurance policies can be tax-deductible if the life policy is owned by a captive insurance company. This is simply not the case. Life insurance premiums are generally not tax-deductible and this holds true for life policies owned by a captive.

Life insurance cash values can offer numerous advantages from an investment point of view—safety of principal, competitive rates of return, guaranteed features from highly rated financial institutions, predicable market values over time, etc. It seems reasonable that a portion of a captive's investment plan could be allocated to cash values providing a safe, guaranteed asset class.

You should take notice that the IRS has not yet provided any guidance on the use of life insurance as part of a captive investment plan. It is reasonable to assume that the IRS may pay increased attention to this topic in the future, if folks abuse the structure. In the event you elect to incorporate life insurance cash values in your captive investment plan, it is absolutely essential that it makes sense as a pure investment allocation decision, and that you consult with your tax advisor and captive management advisory team for guidance.

CHAPTER NINE

LET'S GET STARTED: STEP-BY-STEP GUIDE TO IMPLEMENTING YOUR CAPTIVE

"Synergy—The bonus that is achieved when things work together harmoniously."

- Mark Twain,
Great American Author

The decision to form a captive insurance company should closely resemble the prudent decision making process for the establishment of any new business enterprise. We recommend that you work with your financial and legal advisors to help determine the essential elements critical to successful captive design, formation and ongoing management of your captive.

The insurance regulators in your chosen domicile will require that you enlist a team of specialists to provide the expertise needed to help develop a long-term plan which includes initial implementation and ongoing management of your captive. We found that by putting together a "Best-in-Class" team, your captive insurance company will benefit from retaining the services of several different independent service providers including captive manager,

captive manager, consulting actuary and legal team. During this process, your team will begin to develop an appropriate business and investment plan for your captive.

4. Choose a Domicile

You've decided to build the house ... but, in which neighborhood? As we reviewed in Chapter 4, domicile selection is one of the most important factors to consider when forming a captive insurance company. Items to consider when selecting the most appropriate domicile will include: taxation, regulation, infrastructure, compliance, investment objectives and overall reputation of the domicile and its related structure. It is advantageous to work with a captive advisory team that is domicile neutral, meaning they have the ability to implement captives in multiple domiciles. For example, our expert team of advisors has the regulatory relationships, experience and knowledge to assist in the selection of the most appropriate domicile to generate the most favorable risk management, compliance, profitability, tax and legal results. Let's start building!

"It is the job that is never started
that takes longest to finish. "

- J.R.R. Tolkien,
English Author

5. Complete a Feasibility Study

What is a feasibility study and why do I need one? Every house needs a foundation. The feasibility study is a necessary tool that is intended to identify if your captive structure is viable and able to withstand the financial risks it assumes. The study begins with an overview of your captive, providing the insurance regulators with a summary of the policy form you intend to use, coverage, limits, deductibles, retention, etc. It will also include an analysis of the relevant data including: anticipated premiums, expenses, loss projections, capitalization adequacy and a pro forma financial statement. In a word, the feasibility study is really a measure of the degree of confidence the actuary has for your captive insurance company.

6. Behind the Scenes—Coordinated Underwriting

A coordinated effort is now underway, as your professional advisory team works together to develop your captive's business plan, investment plan, craft your feasibility study and determine the most attractive ownership structure. As you can see, there are many moving parts to attend to. The implementation team is working diligently to refine your structure and tie up any loose ends in order to prepare your captive for submission to the insurance regulatory team for review. The captive manager is obtaining a tax identification number and setting up a bank account. The legal team is working with you and your advisors to further develop and finalize the organizational and legal structure of your captive. They are working together to assemble the required documentation necessary to form your captive in the chosen domicile.

7. Application Process

The bricks and mortar are setting, so let's talk about the paperwork. The captive manager and legal team will send out packages that include the documentation required to submit for the approval of your captive. This will vary from domicile to domicile but you can expect the packages to include a formal application, biographical affidavit and a request for financial information from each prospective owner. Typically, each jurisdiction will assess an application fee. Completing the pertinent paperwork and returning along with the application fee and required capital and surplus payment is essential to getting your captive approved in a timely fashion.

8. Regulatory Approval

You're almost home! The captive manager has submitted the necessary materials for review by the insurance regulatory team in your chosen domicile. They will inspect the application, business plan, investment plan, actuarial study, financial statements and documents to support the ownership structure to determine valid business purpose of the proposed captive. Upon determination from the insurance regulatory team that the requirements have been met, a Certificate of Authority or similar proof of approval is granted on behalf of your captive, giving it the green light to operate as an insurance company.

9. Closing

It's time to make it official. Now that the required entities have been formed and capitalized, and have received a formal approval from the insurance regulatory team, a formal closing may take place according to the regulations of your chosen jurisdiction. The closing process is necessary to complete the implementation of your captive program, especially to allow issuance and delivery of your captive's insurance policies.

Oftentimes, it is a requirement to attend the formal closing. Some domiciles will permit you to appoint an Attorney-in-Fact to represent you at this meeting if you are unable to attend in person.

Congratulations, you are ready to move in!

CHAPTER TEN

PLANNING OPPORTUNITIES

> "There is one and only one responsibility
> of business: to use its resources and engage
> in activities designed to increase its profits so long
> as it stays within the rules of the game."

> – **Milton Friedman,**
> American Economist

Now that your captive insurance company is operational, let's take a look at some of the objectives you can accomplish with it. This chapter is not intended to identify each and every possible planning opportunity because the options are nearly endless.

A captive is a risk management device that, if managed successfully, can result in profits to the owner. Planning will enable the owner to achieve a variety of financial objectives in addition to helping manage risk exposure. As we've discussed in earlier chapters, your captive insurance company is—first and foremost—a structure designed with risk management as its primary business purpose. Successful operation of your captive cannot only help you manage your risk exposure but can also result in significant accumulation of surplus and profits, which can be of value to any business owner. Properly structuring the ownership of your captive can help you utilize the surplus and profits to accomplish a variety of financial objectives.

As we mentioned in the last chapter, one of the important steps in the implementation process is the coordinated effort that occurs behind the scenes. Your professional advisory team will work with you to determine the most attractive ownership structure for your captive. The form of ownership will be influenced by and based upon your financial objectives and the recommendations of your personal advisory team. Flexible ownership options can solidify the numerous advantages of ancillary planning, helping you to achieve secondary financial goals and objectives in addition to the obvious risk management purpose.

Who should own your captive insurance company? Well, it depends. For example, let's say that your captive has been in business for 10 years and has successfully accumulated $10 million in surplus and profits. Precisely what would you like to do with that money? If you were the owner of the captive, your options would be similar to the owner of any successful business with retained earnings on the corporate balance sheet. As owner of the business, you would have access to the accumulated surplus and profits, subject to prevailing tax rates on corporate distributions at that time, after having received approval from the insurance department regulatory team.

Some examples of captive ownership structures are as follows:

- Business or parent operating company
- Owner(s) of the business
- Key employees of the business
- LLC, limited partnership, irrevocable insurance trust
- Spousal access trust
- Generation-skipping irrevocable trust
- Asset protection trust

Ownership of your captive insurance company can ultimately help you to accomplish numerous planning opportunities, typically providing some elements of wealth accumulation, efficient and tax-advantaged wealth transfer and asset protection.

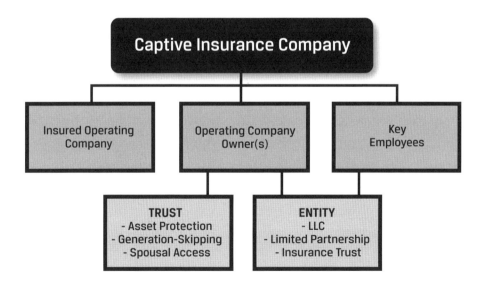

Remember, your captive is a stand-alone business entity that offers many planning advantages to its owner(s) including:

- Additional balance sheet asset for your operating company
- Additional personal balance sheet asset
- Asset protection
- Business succession planning
- Estate planning

Let's look at an example in which the captive is owned by the business or parent operating company. In this design, you would work with your planning team to designate the captive as a wholly-owned subsidiary of the parent company. In the event the captive accumulates surplus and profits over time, assets held in the captive's investment plan on its balance sheet would generate additional capital on the consolidated financial statement of the business. This can be advantageous to community banks looking to build additional regulatory capital to satisfy banking regulators. Construction companies forming captives as wholly-owned subsidiaries can build additional balance sheet liquidity to help meet the requirements of their bonding companies. We have worked with many business owners who found it advantageous to accumulate captive assets to improve their financial statements in support of an existing bank line of credit, loan covenants, buy-sell funding, employee benefit expense exposure or insulate themselves from potentially volatile bank and lending climates.

Alternatively, you may prefer to structure ownership of your captive so that its assets are held off-balance sheet. This could prove beneficial in the event the operating company were to become insolvent or subject to judgment creditor claims.

If you do not believe you will need access to captive surplus, it may make sense to consider an ownership strategy designating an irrevocable trust as owner of your captive. Assuming the entity is created so that it is outside of your taxable estate, your captive can be an effective component of your overall estate plan, without adversely impacting your existing wealth transfer or gifting arrangements.

Examples of such planning can be accomplished through the use of an irrevocable trust, family limited partnership, dynasty trust or generation-skipping trust. In some cases, it may be desirable for ownership to reside with your adult children directly, provided they are over the age of 21. You should look to your estate planning attorney to ultimately provide guidance as to the best mechanism to achieve your estate planning objectives, in coordination with your captive advisory team.

What risks keep you up at night? If you are concerned about the adverse impact of a litigation event and the subsequent attack on your assets, you might want to consider ownership of your captive within an asset protection trust. In today's litigious society, many business owners could face attack from judgment creditors and potential litigants on numerous levels. Asset protection planning could be a key part of your captive strategy as well. By forming your captive within an asset protection trust, you could potentially accumulate a pool of capital that could prove to be extremely difficult for a judgment creditor to gain access to. We have helped to bring additional peace of mind to many physicians, athletes, financial professionals and business owners utilizing this powerful tool.

Estate Planning with a Captive

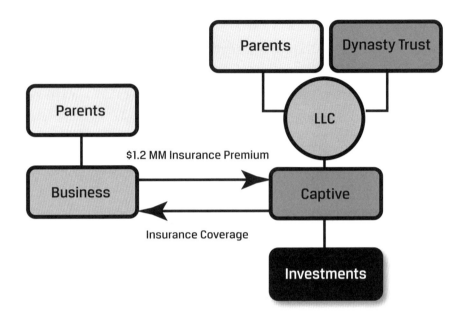

There are numerous additional planning opportunities available to you, which you should review and consider with your captive advisory team members. You should also be sure to include your legal, tax and other professional advisors in the discussion so that the design of your captive insurance company is consistent with your overall plans and objectives.

CHAPTER ELEVEN

FREEDOM OF CHOICE: ADDITIONAL OPPORTUNITIES AND EXIT STRATEGIES

" Destiny is no matter of chance.
It is a matter of choice. It is not a thing to be
waited for, it is a thing to be achieved. "

- **William Jennings Bryan,**
Leading American Politician

Ok, you made it to the home stretch! Everyone on the captive advisory team performed admirably and your captive has been operating successfully for a number of years. You have done a good job maintaining reasonable expenses. Your loss control and claims management initiatives have paid off. The professional investment advisors have generated favorable investment results. All is good.

Your captive insurance company has accumulated significant profit and surplus over the years and you are now wondering, "what can I do with the money, what is the best exit strategy for me?" While you may be asking about potential exit strategies, what you really may be thinking is "when can I do what I want with the surplus that builds inside my insurance company?" This is a good question, asked by anyone who has operated a successful business interest over time. There are many opportunities available to you in addition to flexible options to unwind your captive insurance company.

It is not unusual for the owners of a captive insurance company to utilize accumulated earnings and surplus to build upon their original business plan. For example, our clients often own more than one successful business and they can consider expanding the risks insured by their captive to other companies they operate. Perhaps they can identify additional self-insured risks to incorporate into their policy. Or they may be able to use their captive to absorb additional layers of coverage, allowing them to increase the deductibles on existing commercial insurance policies.

For example, we recently worked with a client who has a very successful business in the financial services industry and was in the process of renewing his captive insurance coverage for the upcoming year. His captive insurance company had been successful and carried significant surplus on the captive balance sheet. During the renewal meeting he identified three additional important risks he wanted to cover. We worked with the captive manager and the consulting actuary on how to best accomplish this request, provided current pricing for the new policy and elected to modify his policy to provide coverage for three additional risks. This example illustrates how your own captive insurance company can create flexible solutions to cover the risks of your operating company as it grows and changes.

Another attractive alternative is for you to consider ways to build upon the profitability of your captive by expanding your investment plan. As we noted earlier, your captive insurance company investment plan provides general guidelines intended to assure safety and liquidity. Certainly, reserves should be invested very conservatively to allow for needed liquidity. As your captive grows larger and continues to accumulate surplus, many captive owners will restructure the investment plan to include real estate, commodities or other alternative investments.

The notion of expanding the investment plan to include a wide range of assets is not unusual. Traditional commercial insurers maintain prudent, well-diversified portfolios. Insurance companies may elect to acquire other companies, typically when they believe they can leverage capacity or management expertise to build more profitability. Some insurance companies, like Berkshire Hathaway, invest in an even more diverse range of companies:

> " The company is known for its control by investor Warren Buffett, who is the company's chairman and CEO. Buffett has used the "float" provided by Berkshire Hathaway's insurance operations (paid premiums which are not held in reserves for reported claims and may be invested) to finance his investments. In the early part of his career at Berkshire, he focused on long-term investments in publicly quoted stocks, but more recently he has turned to buying whole companies. Berkshire now owns a diverse range of businesses including confectionery, retail, railroad, home furnishings, encyclopedias, manufacturers of vacuum cleaners, jewelry sales, newspaper publishing, manufacture and distribution of uniforms, as well as several regional electric and gas utilities." [2]

---

2. "Berkshire Hathaway" Wikipedia

As you can see, it can make a lot of sense for you to take advantage of solid investment opportunities as part of your captive insurance company strategic plan allowing you the freedom to invest in business opportunities where your expertise can be used to create a stronger balance sheet for your captive.

From time to time, it may become apparent that the domicile you originally selected may no longer be the most attractive jurisdiction for your captive. This does not mean that you made a mistake when you established your captive but rather could be the result of turnover in the insurance regulatory team, leading to misalignment with the goals for your particular captive. In the domestic arena, it is not unusual for insurance commissioners to remain on the job for approximately 18 months, resulting in the potential for an inconsistent regulatory environment.

There's an old saying "let's not throw the baby out with the bathwater," which can apply in this situation. If you need a change in venue it does not mean that you must shut down your captive. If the domicile has become less attractive due to regulatory personnel change, inconsistent regulatory environment, increased operational costs, etc., it may make sense to explore alternative domiciles for your captive.

Our captive management team can provide guidance on the selection of alternative jurisdictions and work with you to re-domicile your captive insurance company in a more favorable location. This is another advantage of utilizing a Best-in-Class independent team that has the ability to represent you in numerous domiciles.

You may be wondering, "What happens to my captive if I sell my operating company or go out of business?" Even if the company the captive originally insured is sold, your captive can provide insurance for other entities you own, or a new entity you form. If there is a gap during which you do not have a business that needs to be insured, your captive can elect to become dormant, meaning no premium would be paid for that year and no coverage would be issued by your captive insurance company. While your captive still remains subject to regulatory oversight, its assets can be invested without being exposed to direct or third-party risks.

In the event you become unable or unwilling to continue to utilize your captive insurance company for risk management purposes, you can consider relinquishing your insurance license, followed by merger with a non-insurance company. You would consider this course of action if you believe that the insurance element of the captive is no longer needed and only after consulting with your tax and legal advisors.

As attractive as the above options may be, you may still find that the most attractive course of action is to declare a dividend(s) or simply liquidate the captive. One of the best times to consider potential liquidation options is when you establish your captive. The owner(s) of the captive are the ones who can benefit from dividend distributions, or will be entitled to capital gains treatment upon liquidation, so you need to consider the most appropriate ownership structure for your captive insurance company.

One thing that is certain is that tax laws will continue to change over time, and the only thing we really know is what the tax treatment is today. With that in mind, you may ask, " what options do I have in the event tax rates are unfavorable when I want to have access to the accumulated surplus in my captive?"

The owner of a captive insurance company may choose to borrow from or otherwise pledge accumulated surplus as collateral, subject to approval by the insurance regulatory team in your domicile. As we discussed earlier, the captive should not be used as the owner's personal checkbook. Therefore, any potential loan process should follow established guidelines for such transactions, namely: the demand loan should be adequately documented, an acceptable interest rate should be stated, the interest rate should be based on applicable federal rates published by the U.S. Treasury or another rate that can be documented as an arms length rate, loan interest should be paid as specified, and a schedule for the repayment of demand loan principal should be produced.

CHAPTER TWELVE

WHAT IS THE NEXT STEP?

"Before you start some work, always ask yourself three questions—Why am I doing it, What the results might be and Will I be successful? Only when you think deeply and find satisfactory answers to these questions, go ahead."

- Vishnu Gupta,
Teacher, Philosopher and Advisor

Now that you've made it this far, the notion of owning your own insurance company is no longer as mysterious as you may have originally thought. By reading *Discovering Captives,* you have learned that:

- Captives have withstood the test of time. They can be an effective risk management tool designed to cover real risks faced by business owners.

- A captive is a highly regulated insurance company, offering the potential to deliver numerous benefits and significant financial rewards, with very predictable results.

- Forming your own captive insurance company can reduce income taxes paid by your operating company, when its structure is consistent with published IRS "safe harbor" guidance.

- When forming your own captive, you can structure ownership to complement your estate planning and business succession needs while also having the freedom and flexibility to adjust as your needs change.

- There are many decisions to be made in implementing a captive insurance arrangement. It therefore is essential that you surround yourself with a Best-in-Class advisory team that will identify solutions based on your actual needs and manage your captive insurance company in compliance with regulators in your domicile.

We have discussed what a captive is and why you might want to form one. We've looked at common misconceptions and pitfalls to avoid when establishing your own structure. At this stage of the game, you have the knowledge to ascertain proper design elements, how to build a compliant business and investment plan, how to understand the multitude of fee and cost considerations, and how everything fits together.

In a nutshell, there is no longer the possibility that you or your trusted advisor(s) believe this all sounds too good to be true. As we mentioned in the very first chapter, the concept of captive insurance is not new at all. From those London merchants in the 1800's, to British Petroleum and other corporations with multi-national interests in the 1920's, to Youngstown Sheet and Tube Company, to insurance agent Fred Reiss in the 1950's—who created the concept of a wholly-owned or "captive" insurance company—to most Fortune 500 companies and thousands of small companies today, captive insurance companies have stood the test of time.

Not only are captives perfectly legal but also everything about captives is based on U.S. tax law, including very attractive advantages for programs qualifying under Section 831(b). We have already learned that in order to be eligible for the favorable tax treatment we discussed, it is crucial that the captive insurance company be structured and managed as an actual insurance company, providing true risk, for appropriate premium levels. Your captive insurance company must be organized and operated for bona fide business purposes and demonstrate both risk-shifting and risk-distribution in order for the arrangement to meet IRS requirements to qualify as insurance.

> "Sometimes the questions are complicated and the answers are simple."
>
> - Dr. Seuss

Fortunately, there is a long history of case law and guidance spanning many decades to guide the captive implementation and regulatory team throughout the process; thereby enabling the experts to design a compliant captive insurance company. Better yet, through the application of "safe harbor" guidance, you have a clear path for design, implementation and ongoing management to help your captive insurance company deliver predictable results.

We hope you enjoyed reading this book. Our team would be delighted to work with you and your professional advisors to explore this exciting opportunity further.

APPENDIX A:

NOTES FOR YOUR CFO, CPA OR FINANCIAL ADVISOR

Chapters 1 through 12 were written to provide the reader with a thorough understanding of what a captive insurance company is and how it works without getting too deep into technical underpinning, revenue rulings and the like. This section is intended to provide a more detailed overview of the various technical and accounting considerations involving the decision to consider a captive insurance company for your client.

A captive insurance company is a property and casualty company that is formed to insure the business risks of an operating company, or a combination of brother-sister operating companies. There are many captives in existence to insure numerous types of business and operating company insurance risks. Larger captives managing billions of dollars of assets are formed by Fortune 500 companies to insure their worldwide operations and the primary risks of employee benefits, workers' compensation and health insurance. There are industry specific captives such as oil and gas distributor associations issuing coverage to supplement the primary lines of a distributor's truck transportation liability for accidents. Also, there are industry specific captives for hospitals and the medical industry to insure for malpractice and liability exposures.

There are also captives designed to insure the business enterprise risks of an operating company, which are the type of high-level risks that, while not occurring often, represent exposure to the operating company and its specific type of industry. Captives insuring business enterprise risks are most often formed as a Section 831(b) small captive insurance company and are generally not designed to replace an operating company's primary lines of property and casualty coverage.

The type of captive that Oxford implements for clients is designed to insure the business enterprise risks of an operating company. An IRC Section 831(b) captive with Oxford is not designed to replace the operating company's primary lines of property and casualty coverage. The actuarial underwriters working with Oxford will design coverage to supplement the primary lines of an operating company's property and casualty coverage. Depending on the industry, some coverage examples through a captive with Oxford could include risks associated with legislative and regulatory changes, supply chain interruption, loss of contract, loss of license or certification, loss of key client and reputation risk.

Key elements of forming a captive include the documentation of business purpose and the risk management needs of an operating company. The professionals at Oxford will extensively discuss the business operations and related industry exposures of a company with the owner of a company as well as the company CFO, the independent CPA, and legal counsel. These discussions and the selection of business enterprise risks the company desires to insure are the primary requirements for documenting business purpose and risk management needs of an operating company. Business purpose and risk management needs are further documented in the entity formation legal work, a formal actuarial report and in the submission package for approval by a regulator.

The elements of "risk-shifting" and "risk-distribution" must be present in a captive insurance company structure in order to document that the policy risks are "insurance" risks for federal tax purposes. In Helvering v. LeGierse, the Supreme Court stated that "insurance" requires "risk-shifting" (from the insured's perspective) and "risk-distributing" (from the insurer's perspective). These factors—risk-shifting and risk-distributing—have been named in court cases as well as pronouncements by the IRS, as elements of determining that an arrangement is "insurance." "Risk-shifting" means one party shifts the risk of loss to another and "risk-distributing" means that the party assuming the risk distributes the potential liability, in part, among others.

Risk-shifting involves the transfer of the impact of a potential economic loss from the insured to the insurer. In Revenue Ruling 2008-8, the IRS provided the definition that "Risk-shifting occurs if a person facing the possibility of an economic loss transfers some or all of the financial consequences of the potential loss to the insurer, such that a loss by the insured does not affect the insured because the loss is offset by the insurance payment."

In the typical captive insurance arrangement, there exists an ownership relationship between the operating company and the captive insurance company. The question can arise as to whether the insured has shifted the risk of an economic loss to the captive insurance company given the ownership relationship between the two parties. Fortunately, there are a number of cases in which the courts have held that if a captive insurance company underwrites a significant amount of risks from "unrelated parties," then the element of risk-shifting has been satisfied for insurance purposes.

In 2002, the IRS issued Revenue Ruling 2002-89 in which it offered guidance on the appropriate level of unrelated business that an insurer must have to allow for adequate risk-shifting. The IRS concluded that a captive insurer with more than 50% unrelated business had sufficient risk-shifting to constitute insurance for Federal income tax purposes. As a consequence, the IRS has effectively announced through Revenue Ruling 2002-89 that more than 50% of unrelated business amounts to a "safe harbor" determination of risk-shifting. You must bear in mind that risk-shifting also considers capitalization, reasonableness of premiums and aggregate exposure.

Risk-distributing means that a party assuming the risk distributes his potential liability, in part, among others. In Revenue Ruling 2008-8, the IRS stated, "Risk-distribution necessarily entails a pooling of premiums, so that a potential insured is not in significant part paying for its own risks." The courts have held that where a captive insurer insured several separate, but related, corporations and the losses could be spread among entities within the affiliated group of companies, sufficient risk-distribution existed.

The three Revenue Rulings issued in 2002 are the best pronouncements by the IRS on what constitutes risk-distribution. In Revenue Ruling 2002-89, the IRS concluded that the requisite risk-distribution was present, but the facts did not state how the unrelated risks and premiums were distributed among the unrelated insureds.

The IRS provided further specific guidance in Revenue Ruling 2002-90, which addressed a brother-sister captive insurance company arrangement. The IRS held that a brother-sister captive insurance arrangement would be treated as insurance for federal income tax purposes despite the absence of risks of unrelated parties being insured by the captive. The ruling involved a parent holding company with 12 domestic operating subsidiaries. The parent operating company formed a wholly-owned domestic insurance company to insure the risks of the 12 operating subsidiaries. The IRS found that each subsidiary's risks were distributed through the pooling of premiums of all 12 subsidiaries and that adequate risk-distribution was present. The IRS thus held that the brother-sister arrangements constituted insurance for federal income tax purposes.

The implementation of several captive insurance company arrangements in the Oxford structure have been formed between brother-sister affiliated groups to achieve risk-shifting and risk-distribution within the affiliated group of companies. An analysis of the risk management needs of these affiliated groups, which included more than 12 operating companies, concluded with the affiliated groups able to meet the IRS "safe harbor" requirements for risk-shifting and risk-distribution pursuant to Revenue Rulings 2002-89 and 2002-90. Accordingly, the affiliated groups constituted their own pooling of risk between the 12 or more operating companies.

The Oxford captive insurance company structures risk-shifting and risk-distribution by stipulating that as claims are approved and paid, that 51% of a paid claim is paid by the unrelated risk pool participants and is apportioned to the participants in the risk pool as unrelated risk. The other 49% of a paid claim is direct risk and is paid by the client-owned captive related to the operating company filing the claim. This sharing of 51% unrelated risk by the unrelated risk pool participants satisfies the IRS "safe harbor" guidance provided in Revenue Ruling 2002-89. Furthermore, the Oxford captive insurance company has a risk pool structure that includes more than 12 unrelated participants to satisfy the IRS "safe harbor" guidance provided in Revenue Ruling 2002-90. It is the accomplishment of risk-shifting and risk-distribution that characterizes the premium payments to the captive insurance company as insurance expense.

A final element of forming a captive insurance company is that of economic substance. As part of the Health Care and Education Reconciliation Act of 2010, Congress enacted new IRC Section 7701(o) which provides that in the case of any transaction to which the common law economic substance doctrine is relevant, such transaction is treated as having economic substance if the transaction changes in a meaningful way (apart from federal income tax effects) the taxpayer's economic position, and the taxpayer has a substantial purpose (apart from federal income tax effects) for entering into such transaction. The Oxford captive insurance company structure is designed to assist clients in documenting the risk management needs of their operating company and their corresponding business purpose in forming their captive. Additionally, the "safe harbor" risk-shifting and risk-distribution accomplished by the pooling arrangement should change in a meaningful way (apart from federal income tax effects) the economic position of the operating company paying insurance premiums to the captive insurance company.

The Oxford captive insurance structure is highly regulated and subject to an annual independent CPA financial statement audit and an annual independent actuarial review. The annual independent CPA financial statement audit and the annual independent actuarial review are performed on a calendar year-end basis.

The tax benefits of the captive are numerous. The premium being paid to the captive is deductible as an insurance expense similar to any other property and casualty insurance premium. Accordingly, there is a tax benefit of deducting the premium on the financial books of the operating company.

The captive insurance company is automatically defaulted to and is taxed as a C corporation for federal income tax purposes. The captive elects to be treated as a C corporation, obtains a Federal Tax ID number, and is responsible for filing an annual Form 1120PC income tax return. The captive also elects pursuant to Section 831(b) to be treated as a small insurance company for tax purposes. A small insurance company can receive annual premium income of $1.2 million or less. The tax benefit to the small captive C corporation is that the net premium income is permanently not taxable for federal income tax purposes. Additionally, Delaware captives are subject to a small premium tax of 0.2% and are not currently subject to any other state or local taxes.

The small captive is taxed on its net investment income, after apportioning business expenses directly related to investment income, of the captive. The investment plan of a captive is liquid in nature and can be very broad based. The captive is required by the Department of Insurance to maintain 20% of its annual premium in a cash account. The remaining assets may be invested according to the investment plan. We often see investment plans include municipals or municipal bond funds to generate tax-free income at the C corporation level, high dividend paying stocks to generate the 70% dividends-received deduction on the C corporation tax return, mutual funds, guaranteed annuities and precious metals such as gold bullion. Depending on the captive insurance company structure, a client can direct his investment plan through his investment advisor of choice.

Ownership of a captive insurance company is generally very flexible. The captive can be owned by an individual, an asset protection trust, or an irrevocable trust. Many of our clients have their captives formed within an asset protection trust for creditor protection. Other clients who are planning estates with estate tax consequences often have their captives formed within an irrevocable trust. The captive owned by an irrevocable trust is building wealth outside of the taxable estate and can benefit children, grandchildren and even future generations.

Captive ownership can also be structured as a direct subsidiary of the operating company. Oxford has structured numerous captive insurance company arrangements whereby a C corporation parent operating company owns the captive insurance company as a wholly-owned subsidiary. Often, the reasons for the direct ownership in the captive may involve the fact that the parent operating company has many shareholders such as investor related shareholders; or, a community bank might consider a captive subsidiary due to the number of unrelated shareholders in the bank. Additionally, some C corporation parent operating companies may have banking obligations or construction bonding requirements which render the necessity to have the captive insurance company structured as a wholly-owned subsidiary.

A C corporation can use its balance sheet liquidity to pay a premium to the captive subsidiary and, basically, move the liquidity from the balance sheet of the C corporation parent operating company to the balance sheet of the wholly-owned captive subsidiary. The annual/cumulative benefit is the tax savings of the insurance expense, net of fees and claims experience of the captive. Even better, when the C corporation parent receives cash dividends from its captive subsidiary, the C corporation parent will not pay any corporate income tax on the dividend from the wholly-owned subsidiary pursuant to the consolidated income tax return elimination regulations or the 100% dividends-received deduction pursuant to Section 243.

The discussion regarding parent-subsidiary captive insurance company arrangements can also apply to an S corporation parent operating company with liquidity on the balance sheet. The S corporation parent operating company may contemplate owning the captive as a wholly-owned subsidiary for the same reasons cited above. The primary difference with the S corporation scenario is that the dividends from the captive subsidiary will flow through to the S corporation shareholders as qualified dividends.

We trust you have found this section to be beneficial and look forward to answering any questions you may have.

APPENDIX B:

HISTORY AND KEY COURT RULINGS

Relevant IRS guidance includes the following revenue rulings:

Revenue Ruling 78-338
The Internal Revenue Service held that a Group Captive Insurance Company—where no shareholder's individual risk exceeded 5% of the total risks of the captive—had sufficient risk-shifting and risk-distribution.

Revenue Ruling 2001-31
The IRS abandoned its "economic family theory" with respect to captive insurance transactions.

Revenue Ruling 2002-89
Provides a "safe harbor" determination on the appropriate level of unrelated business that a subsidiary insurer must have to allow for adequate risk-shifting. More than 50% of unrelated business constitutes a "safe harbor" determination of risk-shifting.

Revenue Ruling 2002-90
Reviews brother and sister operating subsidiaries and establishes the Rule of 12 for "safe harbor" purposes.

Revenue Ruling 2002-91

If the liability of each company is no more than 15% of total risks insured by the captive, significant risk-shifting and risk-distribution exists.

Revenue Notice 2004-65

The IRS stated that 831(b) no longer should be identified as "listed transactions" for purposes of disclosure, registration, and list-maintenance requirements.

Revenue Ruling 2005-40

Reviewed cases in which the captive underwrote a significant amount of third-party risks, risk-distribution and risk-shifting were found to be present, even when the captive insurance companies were wholly owned, or nearly wholly owned, by its insured's. For the purpose of the Rule of 12, disregarded entities do not count as separate insureds.

Revenue Ruling 2008-8

The IRS stated "Risk-distribution necessarily entails a pooling of premiums, so that a potential insured is not in significant part paying for its own risks."

Revenue Notice 2008-19

The IRS indicated it intended to set forth proposed guidance on when a protected cell company would be treated as an insurance company.

Proposed Regulations (REG-119921-09)

On September 14, 2010, the Treasury proposed that the individual series within domestic series organizations (typically a series limited liability company—Series LLC) would be treated as a separate entity formed under local law and general tax principles.

Case law impacting business owners who created captive insurance companies began in the early 1900's. This long-standing history of court decisions provides us with a roadmap to allow successful implementation of a captive insurance company, with predictable tax results. Here are some of the key court rulings:

Helvering v. LeGierse (1941)
Established the principle that both risk-shifting and risk-distribution are requirements for a contract to be treated as insurance.

Crawford Fitting Co. v. U.S. (1985)
Insurance premiums paid to a captive by a group of separate corporations that were owned and controlled by a group of related individuals were deductible. The shareholders of the captive were not so economically related that their transactions had to be aggregated and treated as the transactions of a single taxpayer.

Humana, Inc. v. Com'r (1989)
Held that the brother-sister captive arrangement constituted insurance and premium payments of the captive's brother-sister entities (but not its parent) were deductible.

Ocean Drilling & Exploration Company (1991)
Deduction allowed for premiums paid to a captive that was a wholly owned subsidiary based on the following facts: 1) The insured faced recognized hazards. 2) Insurance contracts were written and premiums paid. 3) Unrelated parties purchased insurance. 4) Premiums charged were based on the commercial rates. 5) The company's capitalization was adequate.

Kidde Industries, Inc. v. U.S. (1997)

The court held that premium payments made by brother-sister entities to the captive were currently deductible. Payments made by divisions of the parent corporation did not constitute insurance premiums deductible under IRC §162.

The Harper Group v. Com'r (1992)

Risk-shifting and risk-distribution were present where the captive received 29% to 32% of its premiums from unrelated parties. The captive arrangement was found to constitute insurance and payments made to the captive were deductible.

Sears, Roebuck and Co. and Affiliated Corporations v. Commissioner (1992)

The court recognized that the premiums were determined at "arms length". 99.75% of premiums paid to Allstate came from unrelated insureds. The IRS's "economic family" argument was rejected.

United Parcel Service v. Com'r (2001)

The tax court sided with UPS based on the economic-substance doctrine.